CONDITIONS
OF
LIGHT

Emmanuel Hocquard

CONDITIONS
OF
LIGHT

Elegies

———

Translated by
Jean-Jacques Poucel

LA PRESSE 2010

IOWA CITY & PARIS

Conditions de lumière copyright © 2007 P.O.L éditeur
Translation copyright © 2010 Jean-Jacques Poucel

Published in the United States by La Presse, an imprint of Fence Books

La Presse/Fence Books are distributed by University Presses of New England.
www.upne.com
www.lapressepoetry.com

Library of Congress Cataloguing in Publication Data
Hocquard, Emmanuel, 1940 —
Translated from the French by Jean-Jacques Poucel
Conditions of Light/Emmanuel Hocquard
p.   cm.
ISBN 1-934200-19-0
ISBN 13 978-1-934200-19-3

1. French poetry. 2. Poetry. 3. Contemporary translation.

Library of Congress Control Number: 2009913149

First Edition
10 9 8 7 6 5 4 3 2 1

This book was first published in French in 2007 by P.O.L;
we would like to thank Paul Otchakovsky-Laurens and
the author for permission to publish this translation.

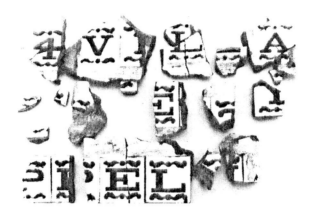

—*All that money lost, where does it go?*
—*It goes nowhere.*

Michelangelo Antonioni, *The Eclipse*

CONDITIONS
OF
LIGHT

I

Until the interlaced bodies
reach the same temperature
Solution of gestures and
speeds
What is being aimed

There are no memories
The smell of burning reeds
in the 40s that Sunday going
down the stairs
   Symmetrical photographs

Opening   without   pre-
position   The gaze escapes the
body   Revolves a door of air
The heat is the event
   Red suits you well

Nights of ago   To love
by definitions   Words in any
given order   Thinking of
separates
To surrender to loss

An image is captivating
You know   To show   Lay
bare   Stairs whose steps don't
follow
Expose your color

CONDITIONS
OF
LIGHT

II

What was seen   *In passing*
Inverted possessive   Long ago
you   also   went   to   school
Black and white flagstones
    Generations of noise

Calendar of earth etched
with a nail into the street
Photograph   *Harem*   *women*
Small glass closure
Where light comes

Lucretius coins the word
vitrum for glass   All things
with similar qualities are the
same
    The lip curves

Revelation recaps it The
attribute   incorporates   the
subject   That's how it is
A babouche turns yellow
    Date-shaped receptacle

Young Woman Reading in a
pale leather chair   Your body
of America   You could say
the name
    Speaking of which

CONDITIONS
OF
LIGHT

III

There   are   no   more
metaphors   *H* is the letter of
the door   Calendar of surfaces
or garden contained
     Back to the wall

The day's trait   Kicking and
screaming   Lines of dirt
Counting by subtraction Given
the weather
    Scratched insistence

Description of the under-
lying questions   Clarity of iris
The third wall or the door
laid out
Entrance & exit

To raise a question in its
place   Two grows by getting
smaller   Light between "to have
in common"
        Separated evaporation

Conjugate with body   The
list is welcoming   Manual
passages   The book opens
Light enters
    A table in mid-air

CONDITIONS
OF
LIGHT

IV

Surfaces slide under others
by contagion   Small grate
opening   You can't see
the corner
The object on display

Color is neutral   Between
equals a dress   Retained letters
Put forward   Without saying
a thing
How to go about

Earth turns to water   Milk
can't be a mirror   Under the
influence of sun glass becomes
fire
As do eyes

Across from   The image
absorbs light   Parts of the body
without reciprocity   To think
by destination
        The back sees

Facing the light   To be
struck   The back-lit visitor
flooded with light   There had
not been someone
    Skin is white

CONDITIONS
OF
LIGHT

V

I recall the iron gates and
the tears   At the right angle
The sight of discordant accords
The main post office
    Iridescence is feminine

An   inaccessible   invention
A kitchen basket   An unlikely
proof   When cork remains
on the surface
      Banana trees flower

Question of bench   Several
layers on the threshold   The
discovery of mica and gypsum
Every time
     Oranges by compass

Fresh bread has a pleasant
smell   The plate falls   What
do rabbits do   Watch a black
cloud passing
    Complete the rain

Lightning   Whirlwinds of
particles   Thunder   Rain
He   looks   at   her   a   long
time
Red-seeded fruit

CONDITIONS
OF
LIGHT

VI

You recognize it all   You
know the words   The lamp
shines down upon the paper
The light falls on
    A breast comes out

The ass brays   Now it
is written   Small museum of
things mistaken   Painted clay
toys
   Street in the sun

A seamless and wordless
album of exceptions   So
wash just below the water
Flat bottom fish
A willow branch

Linens dry fast   Out of
sight of land   Initials carved
into the formica of a table
on deck
    He doesn't get better

The film is medium speed
The reflector is a white piece
of cardboard   The light here is
beautiful
Without makeup

CONDITIONS
OF
LIGHT

VII

Always   the   same
snapshot   Something not yet
embodied   Mango bubble
bath
    In red light

Wet   hair   appears   darker
When   paper   soaks   up
the   daylight   syllables
go black
    Building the rule

Pre-statue factory   Arms
crossed between rows of aloe
and the sea   Small war fleet
for the sinking
    It's just starting

The crates are empty but
the light is there   A broad sun
broadens the page   Endless
exposure time
    I see you say so what

You must not say what
a silence   You must say I can't
hear   The propositions must
be washed in fresh water
    A lightwell

CONDITIONS
OF
LIGHT

VIII

The school girl packs her
book bag   Your body is the
telling   My focus is luminous
One dream at a time
    It's no one's fault

What they have in common
does not communicate   A set
square   A castaway's fire
Apricot pits
Abduction from the Seraglio

It backfires   That animal
smiled at me then bit   Sleeping
together is learned alone   A life
of labels
    Nothing but the facts

8 impasse du chien or the
street number   An arrow
sows doubt   Pain can't be
localized
        Until below the surface

A   series   of   unhingings
The territory is hidden   If
there were a strike   Suddenly
look beyond
    The missing map

CONDITIONS
OF
LIGHT

IX

The color and the thing in
one   A moment apart Dia-
logue of blue robins   Both
sides of the postcard
      Perfect bust

What we are calling here is
a brief duration   The weather
is fine here   An interval factory
should suffice
    Eclipse instead of fable

Light   on   the   mouth
The light of your mouth
Vacuole of glass   Between
the reader's hands
    The glass word

Return of the beloved figure
Her strange visitation   Neither
the *story* *so* *far* nor *to* *be*
continued
Beside yourself

Linked   by   juxtaposition
Ordinary weird   The hermit
and the lumberjack   Joy apart
In the gaze of monkeys
No other formula

CONDITIONS
OF
LIGHT

X

Behind the wall or the door
Before & after   Playground
at recess   Bakery & cinema
The dog dreams and sighs
     The everyday

Depleted terrain   A
dimished energy   A set is
indifferent Stopped language
Stained petals
      Clarity of sand

Beauty does not belong any
more   than   sleep   or   hunger
It's the same   When you speak
or when you sleep
    In red minor

Loss of light   Tyranny of
icons and names   Empty
window   Here & there   Who
guards the dead-ends
      Shield of fear

Dis-fixing   She's taken the
town   Sparks in the morning
A knot   I walk this street
for you
     Who is not the question

CONDITIONS
OF
LIGHT

XI

A love of a child   Play
hot   box   or   four   square
in the garage that's no longer
there
Architectural page

Smile in the kitchen   Raise
your eyes   Open your hand
The disorientation that ensues
Touch your soul
    Answer the letter

Please find here attached
my curriculum vitae   It's the
same   My name is he says
And mine she says
    Fists up in sleeves

The words to say them
A violet shirt   Girls on the
terrace   The cat slips between
the washtubs
    Night falls again

A   question   seeks   its
formula   Marmoset fingers
on branches   What do you call
those flowers
    Sidi Walou's mausoleum

CONDITIONS
OF
LIGHT

XII

Speak into a mirror   Flat
angle   Now there is a ravine
And the smell of paint   Where
do things go
    It doesn't matter

Light enters into a relation
of broken alliance   There
is the page and the fly   It is
black
    Two pages

Without caesura   Describe
the house as a calendar of
the garden   Including in turn
Viridarium
　　Postcard box

Encrusted things   A crab
molts   Old book bag all stained
with ink inside   White
words
    Blackboard in a corner

Describe   to   exhaustion
Words stumble over *H*   The
last letter   Such a perspective
has been
       An italic alphabet

CONDITIONS
OF
LIGHT

XIII

During   the   rests   the
reactions   are   characters
Technical   instructions   prove
more sensual

Chronique d'un amour

The emphasis is on the
gaze   The heart and details
The question is what other
form
     Seen from outside

The position of the body is
unlikely   Clothes non-descript
Situation in which inequity is
not at stake
　　Carnivore and cannibal

Copy one hundred times I
must not copy   The night scene
in the bathtub looks like an
investigation
Taking after the makers

After
    the walls of the room
turn pink   The sequence is
edited out
    The factories' curves

CONDITIONS
OF
LIGHT

XIV

A   modern   program
A book donation   The kept
years   What remains for us
of gazing
   Reference to paper

Negative light   The stain
and two spots   transparent
within the surface   The
fascination of maps
    Suspended plans

Meaning   imposes   its
fiction   Cloth snaps in this
language   House of voices or
office of resemblances
    Bodies: deposition 1

Collectible scene   It exists
only for you   Road lined
with poplars   Recourse to
negative exposure
    Blue p.c. 725

It is noon touches the back
In the darkness photos await
The dough rises on the type
shop stool
The very idea of relation

CONDITIONS
OF
LIGHT

XV

Invisible   rules   are   for
mourning   Trees in the trees
The *sea* enters from the *edge*
You see the fabric
    Lion and carburetors

A plane is standing still in
the air   above   the skyscrapers
are flat   You repack the boxes
on the stairs
    You will also see a pond

Glass   contains   its   own
light   Red in green spring
maples   Imagine a fish or its
geometry
     Measure a chair

The relationship between
a noun and its object has not
been found   The *stropper* and
the form in pink glass
     Filing by dynasty

The word defines use   I
saw   my   first   cardinal   in
Brooklyn   It   was   *like*
counting by color
    Or setting your watch

CONDITIONS
OF
LIGHT

XVI

Light & brick are still
beautiful   Words near for
tears   A page torn out or set
apart
     And nothing

At night on the bank
the frogs sing in the trees
Nothing but arrangement
without order
An idea of brass

Ideal conditions of light   In
strokes   "An object affixed at
the threshold"   In the door
that does not open
　You reds

An elementary speech   The
means of erasure   Without the
object red   Nor gathering the
slightest sound
    The words of the title

Until the first has been
exhausted   As person
Desirable person   The surface
of the earth
    Only one opens

CONDITIONS
OF
LIGHT

XVII

The ground reflected white
Arrangement of bodies   Seen
up close   Next to for anew
Sixteen years
    Or these eyes

It is a murder   The line
follows an angle in the finery
Exact birthday of the body
broken habit
    Among conversations

She shows without saying
a thing   Separates water and
stones   An animal falters in the
undertaking
    Trading in waxes

A collection of unfinished
houses   Childhood in the
first   person   Without
surrender
      Definition of the back

I saw the things you did
not know   Visitation   That
mirror and white   Dogs are not
allowed
    Answer uncalled for

CONDITIONS
OF
LIGHT

XVIII

Between door and beneath
A wall of letters   As you were
saying   This a body or this
a sentence   A taste of
    That was possible

We put voice on the table
Sprung   The theme and the
mode   Red spreading out
Something of the cold
    An ever so slow retreat

The sentence on the
envelope   Cricket on it hidden
Surface out of reach His arms
around her waist
What belongs to song

A card in the hollow of the
hand   One day   What would
not change   Set the cup beside
the cup
    Written proof

But color   The gaze of
colors   Rigging severed
by lightning Thinning   Lines
witness the back
      We had said

CONDITIONS
OF
LIGHT

XIX

Four set on water   With no
point of contact   Hands part
the cloth in front   A body
absorbs its own light
    Signs in waves

Sheets barely move   The
claim rooted in the landscape
Give your place to the name
An echo of the plot
    Or breathing in the margins

Sidelined on the same level
Distance is near   Two is
corrected   A trait vanishes
as soon as it appears
        It appears

Past focus   Cockerels see
the day before   Optical traces
of a body from the elbow down
Without outline
    Coloring cause

A   light   brought   back
Objects settle in for the long
run within the frame   Fragment
of characters laid out
    Read and arrange

CONDITIONS
OF
LIGHT

XX

To sleep   shard   in   hand
I   look   at   these   mountains
for you   Body as extended
use
     Folded light

Clothing contaminates the
landscape   A palm tree takes
to   the   sea   Around   a
Description of a sneeze
    Photographic color

Snow   &   prepositions
engage in varied associations
The neighbor's field   In the
absence of proof
Another fold

These flowers are in the
middle of their making   I think
of you   The noise of laundry
Inventing tools and rivers
    Solid white of names

The representation of the
same is just right   Whatever
a witness *says* he saw or heard
A bird book
      In writing

CONDITIONS
OF
LIGHT

XXI

The   tablet   scraped   bare
Soot retains light   Mimosa
archives   Your   enamel
figurines
    Pierced miniature

The possibility of not being
as you are not.   That is
none other   Water the beans
before the rain
    Breathing aside

Day defined by night   Body
by another   In the middle of
arranging   Plurality of roles
and masks
    Speaking statues

Thus doing   Spaces agree:
cockerel voice shard Separate
at the same time   Free
of cause
    Not to

Body   for   phosphorus
The size of an egg   Unstable
display   Noise   contains
its stillness
Without the end

IN GLASS

Propositions are independent
Between them relations take
place   So propositions follow
or attract or repel one another
or sound an echo The narrative
unfolds in these encounters
Should they come to falter
(aporia) a story falls short
  Words are the characters in
the grammatical fable You can
only restate   You recite when
you speak a language   You
can't hear it any further   You
hear only its recitation   I
remember words   I recognize
them   When you say *the sky is
blue* the entirety of language

is contained

Elegy is not in words of
lament   It is in the repetition
of the words of a language   It is
this repetition   Language in its
entirety is elegy

One never speaks of oneself
Never has there been a speaking
subject   The only subject there
is is grammatical There is no
beginning   There is no first
formulation   There is but recol-
lection   In a glass bowl

Simple statements no longer
exist   Every statement is legion
Even   an   isolated   word
resounds   It's the Theater of
language The staging of belief
in Of making believe that   To

dream or make dream that
a first statement is possible
Such a statement would be
unheard and thus inaudible   It
remains that this inaudible is
secretly sought after in what is
said or heard or written The
singular surprise is revealed in
repetition We called it *littéralité*
Littéralité dazzles

Even if one does not
quite understand what has
come to be an unlatching
has occurred   A difference
in intonation and speed
The intonation of the
recitation is neutral   Its
speed constant   An interval
or an exit space has taken

place   For entering never was
the question   In speaking or
writing or reading or translating
one seeks the exit   To escape
    Writing is this opening

NOTES

1. Read omitting the prepositions.

2. Read omitting the verb to be.

3. Read omitting the other verbs.

4. Read each elegy as a list of utterances.

5. Read each page like the text of a postcard.

6. Read in the sun.

7. Read each page twice.

8. Read what is written the way it is printed.

Emmanuel Hocquard is one of the leading poets of post-68 France. His early press, Orange Export Ltd., along with the reading series that he ran at the the Musée d'Art Moderne de la Ville de Paris, helped sculpt the French post-modern poetic sensibility. His extensive influence can be seen in subject matter and syntax through- out the work of two younger generations. The author of over thirty books, his work crosses genres and includes many critical articles, a novel, and a film in addition to his poetry. He has also worked extensively in translation and has been responsible for the reception of many important 20th century American poets in France. In addition to translating works by Charles Reznikoff, Michael Palmer, Paul Auster, and others, he is the founder and co-director, with Juliette Valéry, of "Un Bureau sur l'Atlantique," an organization that fosters French-American poetic exchange. In conjunction with the Abbaye de Royaumont, he ran a series of group translation seminars throughout the eighties and nineties that resulted in French translations of dozens of American poets. He is the co-editor, with Claude Royet-Journoud of two volumes of translation from the American, 21 + 1 poètes américains d'aujoud'hui, and 41 + 1. His work is the subject of a volume in the critical series Poètes d'aujoud'hui pubished by Seghers and is featured in countless works on poetics by Dominique Rabaté, Jean- Marie Gleize, Gilles Tiberghien, and others. His work is attracting increasing attention in the United States; seven full-length volumes have been translated and published, and his work appears online at PENNsound, the Electronic Poetry Center, and durationpress.com. Michigan critic Glenn Fetzer writes, "In his pursuit of literality, Hocquard enacts a model of the "discontinuous organization of language," a poetic practice known to some as an "action poétique." Longtime professor at the school of fine arts in Bordeaux, he lives and works in the south of France.

Jean-Jacques Poucel is associate professor of French literature at Yale University. He is the author of *Jacques Roubaud and the Invention of Memory* (University of North Carolina Press, 2006) and has completed studies on several members of the Oulipo, some of which are published in *Pereckonings: Reading Georges Perec* (*Yale French Studies* 105) and *Constraint Writing* (*Poetics Today* 30: 4 & 31:1), which he guest edited. He is a member of the collective Double Change and an editor-at-large for *Drunken Boat*. He is currently writing a study of French lyric poetry from the nineties to the present. He translates as a means of reading.

This is the sixth title in the La Presse series
of contemporary French poetry in translation.
The cover image is the translator's typescript
with the translator's holographic notes.
The series is edited by Cole Swensen.
The book is set in Adobe Jenson and
was designed by Shari DeGraw.